Multicultural Folk Dance
Guide

Volume 1

Christy Lane
Susan Langhout

Human Kinetics

Library of Congress Cataloging-in-Publication Data

Lane, Christy.
 Multicultural folk dance guide / Christy Lane, Susan Langhout.
  p. cm.
 ISBN 0-88011-905-5 (v. 1). -- ISBN 0-88011-921-7 (v. 2)
  1. Folk dancing. 2. Manners and customs. 3. Folk dancing--Study
 and teaching. I. Langhout, Susan, 1966- . II. Title.
 GV1743.L36   1998
 793.3'1--dc21   98-10648
                                                            CIP

ISBN-10: 0-88011-905-5
ISBN-13: 978-0-88011-905-4

Copyright © 1998 by Human Kinetics, Inc.

Developmental Editor: Judy Patterson Wright, PhD; **Managing Editors:** Lynn M. Hooper-Davenport and Lisa Satterthwaite; **Graphic Designer:** Nancy Rasmus; **Graphic Artist:** Francine Hamerski; **Cover Designer:** Jack Davis; **Printer:** United Graphics

Printed in the United States of America   20   19   18   17   16   15   14   13

The paper in this book is certified under a sustainable forestry program.

Human Kinetics
Web site: www.HumanKinetics.com

United States: Human Kinetics, P.O. Box 5076, Champaign, IL 61825-5076
800-747-4457
email: humank@hkusa.com

Canada: Human Kinetics, 475 Devonshire Road Unit 100, Windsor, ON N8Y 2L5
800-465-7301 (in Canada only)
email: info@hkcanada.com

Europe: Human Kinetics, 107 Bradford Road, Stanningley, Leeds LS28 6 AT, United Kingdom
+44 (0) 113 255 5665
email: hk@hkeurope.com

Australia: Human Kinetics, 57A Price Avenue, Lower Mitcham, South Australia 5062
08 8372 0999
e-mail: info@hkaustralia.com

New Zealand: Human Kinetics, P.O. Box 80, Torrens Park, South Australia 5062
0800 222 062
e-mail: info@hknewzealand.com

The *Multicultural Folk Dance Treasure Chest* (including the booklet, music, and video packages) is dedicated to all the young people in the world. It is hoped that all the diverse cultures that make up this vast and exciting place we live in will be brought together with a better understanding of each other through dance, thus increasing peace and harmony.

CONTENTS

ACKNOWLEDGMENTS

I am grateful to the following individuals who have contributed to this project. First, I would like to acknowledge Rainer Martens for his ability to see the importance of dance in our society and for his insight, vision, and willingness to help young people around the world. My gratitude is extended to Richard Duree, dance ethnologist and historian, for consulting on this project. Sincere thanks to Adrienne Sabo, Margaret Roza, Lynnanne Hanson, Charlie Griswold, Pete and Portia Seanoa, Judith Scalin, Louise Reichlin, Bob Osgood, Elaine Weisman, Char Schade, Jerry Krause, David Rojas, Scot Byars, Francesco Geora, Derrick J. LaSalla, Carlos Vigon, Loyola Marymount University dance department, University of Southern California dance department, City of Los Angeles Cultural Affairs, Aman Folk Ensemble, Highland School District in Burien, Washington, National Dance Association, Westchester Lariats, and all the dancers and teachers who participated in the creation of the *Multicultural Folk Dance Treasure Chest,* for their time, advice, and support of this project. It was a pleasure to work with such a great production team, especially Doug Fink, Roger Francisco, Bobby Morganstein, Rick Hall, Studio West, Mr. Scenic, Snap Lock Company, and the incredible staff at Human Kinetics. Finally, my most sincere appreciation is extended to all the teachers I have met around the country for their inspiration, optimism, and desire to share dance.

Christy Lane

INTRODUCTION

Welcome to the wonderful world of dance! You are about to experience folk dancing, the oldest form of dance. It is the basis for many other dance forms. The term *folk dancing* is usually defined as "the dance of the common people." Just where or when it began is impossible to document. Archaeologists and historians say it was a basic part of early peoples' culture as they used dance to communicate their emotions through movement and rhythm. People have danced and still dance for celebration, for survival, to socialize, to communicate with the spiritual, and to express their membership and identity in communities.

The purpose of this combined video, music, and booklet package is to provide simplified, hands-on tools for those wishing to participate in a meaningful and enjoyable program of folk dance. On the video, each dance is taught by an expert or a native of the country from which the dance originates. The dances have been carefully chosen to provide a successful and meaningful experience to all involved and an optimal mix of cultural diversity and samples for different levels. The dances selected were a result of a nationwide survey. Each dance has appropriate musical accompaniment that was specifically developed for use with the videotape and this booklet. The music was derived from original, authentic compositions of the popular songs used with the selected dances.

Folk Dancing Benefits

This volume gives you an opportunity to learn about nine cultures. Each dance reflects the geography, climate, music, lifestyles, beliefs, and history of a people. It takes on the characteristics of the locale. For example, climate is a factor of great importance. Generally, the dances from frigid climates are quick-moving with strong, vigorous movements and sustained action. Dances from very warm climates have fluid movements and are more flowing and slow. In temperate climates, the dances seem to be more balanced between the vigorous and quiet actions. Mountain dwellers tend to be more isolated and less mobile than those who live in the plains, and their dances tend to be done in one place, while the dances of the people of the plains fly across the floor as though the dancers were riding horseback across the great open plains.

The forms, patterns, and functions of folk dance vary as much as the cultures. The dances can be done with or without partners; in circles, squares, or long lines; in threesomes, foursomes, or alone. As a means of expression, dances such as wedding dances, war dances, contest dances, courtship dances, work dances, religious dances, and special holiday dances have been created.

Folk dancing is very social and recreational in nature. Each dancer is a member of a larger group, and dancers change partners frequently during many of the dances, promoting communication between people who might otherwise be too timid. Folk dancing helps to develop rhythmic movements, neuromuscular coordination, balance, and poise. It is a challenge to learn new skills, and dance allows participants, regardless of their ages, the satisfaction of both achievement and acceptance.

How to Use This Booklet

In this guide, you will find the following information for each of the nine dances:

- Origin
- Location
- Language
- Flag
- Traditional costume
- History
- Difficulty level
- Stance
- Music selection and time signature
- Number of participants
- Formation
- Directions
- Modifications
- Trivia

Selected photographs taken from the video illustrate portions of the dance and show the dancers in action. As appropriate, a diagram is included to show the formation of the dance. You may use the modification suggestions either to simplify the dance or to add variety. The nine dances in this volme are presented in easy-to-difficult order and reflect three degrees of difficulty— easy, moderate, and advanced. The easy dances are shorter and less complex than the advanced dances, which have more intricate steps performed to a faster tempo. Each dance concludes with an interesting bit of trivia to enhance your understanding of the culture.

If you are a teacher, you'll find the For Teachers Only section to be helpful. It includes suggestions for presenting, managing, and introducing dances in order to keep things fun and interesting for all. Lastly, there is a Resources section that identifies the selected dance instructors and lists equipment sources.

Authentic music and rhythm are important in all folk dances. Rhythm is the beat that drives dance movements. It is the musical sound that catches the essential style and quality of the dance. Time signatures of 2/4, 3/4, 4/4, and 6/8 are commonly used in Western cultures. Eastern cultures tend to use irregular meters such as 5/16, 7/8, and 11/16. Both the specific music selection and the time signature are listed per dance. Also, see page 49 of this guide for more information on the companion music and videos available for each volume of dances.

The folk dance experience involves more than performing the steps correctly. It is an opportunity to develop a better understanding of the customs and traditions of other cultures through a nonjudgmental curiosity, and to discover that dance can be a common bond between people of all nations. Folk dance is an expression of the human spirit.

Welcome to an exciting adventure of dance!

Diagram Key

○ = women   □ = men

HORA
(ho'rah)

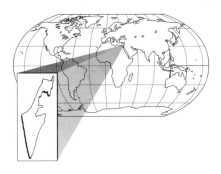

▶ Origin
Israel

▶ Location
Middle East, bordering the Mediterranean Sea, Egypt (in the south), Lebanon (in the north), and Jordan (on the eastern side). The climate of Israel is generally subtropical, with rainfall typically limited to the winter months.

▶ Language
Hebrew is the official language, Arabic is the second language for the Arab minority, and English is taught at all schools from the fourth grade. *Hava nagilah* means "let's celebrate." *Shalom* means "hello," "goodbye," and "peace."

▶ Flag
White background with a blue Star of David (Shield of David) centered between two equal horizontal blue stripes

▶ Traditional Costume
Men wear long tunic tops with pants. Women wear belted mid-calf length dresses with full skirts and colorful scarves around their necks.

▶ History of Dance
The hora, which probably originated in Hungary or Greece, is the national dance of Israel. It is danced at festive occasions, such as weddings and barmitzvahs, and has been performed for many years around the world. It is a symbol of national strength and spirit. The goal

is to join people together in true celebration by joining hands and being together. There are variations being created by many countries.

▶ Difficulty Level
Easy

▶ Stance
Somewhat erect

▶ Music Selection & Time Signature
Hava Nagilah (also spelled Hava Nagila); 4/4 time

▶ Number of Participants
No limit

▶ Formation
Either a single circle or a broken circle, with dancers facing in toward the center and traveling clockwise while holding the hands of the people on either side with arms straight

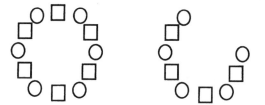

Directions

Eight Total Counts
(Count 1) Step on the left foot to the left side.

(Count 2) Kick the right foot to the left side (in front of left leg).

(Count 3) Step on the right foot to the right side.

(Count 4) Kick the left foot to the right side (in front of right leg).

(Count 5) Step on the left foot to the left side.

(Count 6) Cross the right foot in front of the left foot.

(Count 7) Step on the left foot to the left side.

(Count 8) Cross the right foot in back of the left foot.

Repeat this pattern throughout while traveling clockwise. Add a bounce to each step to make it more lively.

▶ Modifications

- This dance may be performed in six counts by eliminating the seventh and eighth counts.
- To simplify, begin this dance slowly, then continue to pick up speed.
- Instead of holding hands, place hands on shoulders.
- When performed in a broken circle, the leader may either serpentine around the dance area or spiral in toward the center, then reverse the direction to move the broken line counterclockwise to spiral out from the center.
- The formation may be changed by using a double circle, or a circle within a circle.

▶ TRIVIA TIDBITS ◀

- The Dead Sea is the lowest place in the entire world and the only sea no fish live in.
- Before we had ships, the only connection between Africa and Europe was Israel.

HUKILAU
(hoo-kee-lau)

▶ Origin

Hawaii, which was the most recent state to be admitted to the United States when it became the 50th state on August 21, 1959

▶ Location

A group of islands in the Pacific Ocean. There are eight main islands in Hawaii. The major islands in order of size are Hawaii, Maui, Oahu, Kauai, Molokai, Lanai, Niihau, and Kahoolawe.

▶ Language

There are many languages spoken in the islands. However, English and Hawaiian are the most common.

▶ Flag

Eight alternating vertical white, red, and blue stripes with a British Union Jack in the upper-left corner

▶ Traditional Costume

The men wear either a *malo* (loin cloth) or *lava lava* (a piece of material wrapped around the waist, tucked in the side and hung down to mid calf). The women wear *pahu* skirts and tops (gathered skirt that hangs to knees or mid calf with a gathered strapless top that sometimes has sleeves like a peasant blouse) or *muumuu* (baggy dress). Both men and women wear flower *lei*s (flowers sewn together like a necklace) around the neck.

▶ History of Dance

Hukilau translates as "fishing party." It is a fun hula dance that tells the story of having a feast after the fishermen, together with their families, bring their catches in. The fish are caught in huge nets held in the shallow waters, then pulled onto shore. The song words *ama ama* mean "little fishes."

▶ Difficulty Level

Easy

▶ Stance

Loose and easy

▶ Music Selection &Time Signature

Hukilau (4/4 time)

▶ Number of Participants

No limit

▶ Formation

Scattered

Directions

Footwork: Basic Hula Step

(4 counts) Three steps and a touch, or tap, to the right side: Step to the right side with the right foot, step on the left foot (placed next to the right foot), step to the right side with the right foot, and tap the ball of the left foot beside the right foot.

(4 counts) Repeat in opposition beginning with the left foot.

This basic hula step is repeated throughout the entire dance.

Part 1: Hands

(4 counts) Left hand on hip. Right thumb points over right shoulder twice.

(4 counts) Pretend you are grabbing a net on your right side with both hands and pull it toward you twice.

(4 counts) Pretend you are grabbing a net on your left side with both hands and pull it toward you twice.

(4 counts) Pretend you are grabbing a net on your right side with both hands and pull it toward you twice.

(4 counts) Arms cross in front and open to sides.

(4 counts) Arms cross over chest, as if hugging yourself.

(4 counts) Left hand is cupped to make a bowl or plate, right forefinger and middle finger scoop *poi* from the bowl up to the mouth. Repeat.

(4 counts) Throw the net out in front of yourself by extending the hands from the side of the body, palms up to front of body.

(4 counts) Hands in front of waist, make wave motion downward right, left, right, left.

(4 counts) Place one hand on top of the other, palms down, imitating a fish by waving hands forward.

(4 counts) Point to yourself with right thumb.

(4 counts) Left hand on hip. Right thumb points over right shoulder twice.

(4 counts) Pretend you are grabbing a net on your right side with both hands and pull toward yourself twice.

(4 counts) Repeat to your left side.

(4 counts) Repeat to your right side.

Part 2: Hands

(4 counts) With both arms pull the net over the right shoulder and throw out to the front.

(4 counts) Bring left hand to right elbow with right elbow on top of left hand. Bring right arm down away from body.

(4 counts) Right hand to left chest with palm down and elbow lifted. Left hand is on waist.

(4 counts) Repeat with left hand to right chest and right hand on waist.

(4 counts) Palms up with arms extended front.

(4 counts) Turn palms down and pretend you are swishing the nets back and forth.

(8 counts) Turn palms out and make a big circle above waist with arms.

Repeat Part 1 twice.

Ending: Hands

(4 counts) Pretend you are grabbing a net on your left side with both hands and pull it toward you twice.

(4 counts) Pretend you are grabbing a net on your right side with both hands and pull it toward you twice.

(8 counts) Pull three times to the right, with all your might. Then, extend arms out to sides, hands together in front, and bow.

This dance is easier to do if you know the lyrics. The lyrics on the following page are broken down into the same counts as the dance directions!

Modifications

• Start with small portions, and slowly add more movements until each part is learned.

• Increase the difficulty level by performing the arms and at the same time circling the hips. Or, perform the arms while stepping around in a circle.

Part 1: Lyrics

Oh, we're going to a
hukilau
a huki, huki, huki, huki
hukilau.
Everybody loves
a hukilau, where
the laulau is the kaukau at
the big luau
We'll throw our
nets out
into the sea and
all the ama ama come
swimming to me.
Oh, we're going to a
hukilau
a huki, huki, huki, huki,
hukilau

Part 2: Lyrics

What a wonderful day for
fishing
in the old Hawaiian way.
All the hukilau nets
go swishing
down in old Laie Bay.

Repeat Part 1's Lyrics Twice

Ending: Lyrics

huki, huki, huki, huki
hukilau
huki, huki, huki, huki,
hukilau

▶ TRIVIA TIDBITS ◀

- Tahitians use grass skirts; Hawaiians use ti leaves for skirts. The ti leaves are picked fresh for performances, shredded into strands with the fingernails, then tied into cording. They only last a few days.
- The only city whose name can be spelled completely with vowels is Aiea, Hawaii.

SAVILA SE BELA LOZA
(sah-vee'-lah say bay-lah loh'-zah)

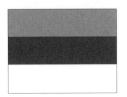

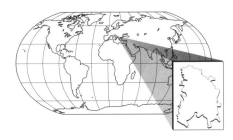

▶ Origin
Serbia

▶ Location
Southeastern Europe, bordering the Adriatic Sea, Albania, Bosnia, and Herzegovina. Serbia was formerly a republic of Yugoslavia.

▶ Language
Serbo-Croatian is the most popular language; however, Albanian is also used.

▶ Flag
Three equal horizontal stripes of blue, white, and red

▶ Traditional Costume
Men wear an embroidered white shirt, gray or black jodhpur-like pants, a woven sash, embroidered knee socks with a moccasin-like shoe (*opanci*), a sleeveless jacket decorated with soutache and a flat cap made of lamb's wool. Women wear an embroidered white linen shift with a woven wool overskirt and apron, a sleeveless bodice decorated with embroidery and soutache, embroidered socks, and opanci.

▶ History of Dance
Savila se bela loza means "a (grape) vine entwined in itself." This is a traditional Serbian line dance, called a *kolo* (wheel), which describes the shape of the dance. Serbian kolos are distinguished by their light and bouncy style.

▶ Difficulty Level
Easy

▶ Stance

Somewhat erect

▶ Music Selection & Time Signature

Savila Se Bela Loza (4/4 time; there is an eight-count introduction)

▶ Number of Participants

No limit

▶ Formation

Single circle or broken circle, with dancers facing in toward the center, hands joined and held low, while moving counterclockwise

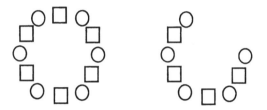

Directions

Part 1: Use 20 Counts to Each Side

(19 counts) Face slightly to the right side. Beginning with the right foot, take 19 small running steps (circle moves counterclockwise).

(1 count) Hop on the right foot.

(19 counts) Face slightly to the left side and repeat the 19 small running steps, beginning with the left foot (circle moves clockwise).

(1 count) Hop on the left foot.

Part 2: Face Middle of Circle (Six Schottische Steps)

(4 counts) Begin with the right foot, and take one schottische step moving right. (Step right, left, right, and hop on the right foot.)

(4 counts) Begin with the left foot, and take one schottische step moving left. (Step left, right, left, and hop on the left foot.)

(4 counts) Repeat schottische with the right foot to the right side.

(4 counts) Repeat schottische with the left foot to the left side.

(4 counts) Repeat schottische with the right foot to the right side.

(4 counts) Repeat schottische with the left foot to the left side.

If you would like to sing the lyrics while dancing, see page 15!

▶ Modifications

- Play the music slowly, then gradually pick up speed.
- Leave out the hop on the schottische during Part 2, and substitute a touch or a tap.
- Perform the dance with hands on hips.
- When performed in a broken circle, the leader may serpentine around the dance area.
- Perform the dance without the bouncy style of run. Substitute with a fast walk.

▶ TRIVIA TIDBIT ◀

- Music and dance have always been a part of every holiday, celebration, and important event throughout the year.

Verse 1: Lyrics

A

Savila se bela loza vinova
Uz tarabu vinova
(repeat two times)
(Repeat A)

A pretty grapevine entwined itself
Along a fence, a grape (vine)

B

Todor Todi podvalio
Triput curu poljubio
(Repeat B twice)

Todor tricked Toda
Kissed the girl three times

Verse 2: Lyrics

A

To ne bese bela loza vinova
Uz tarabu vinova
(repeat two times)
(Repeat A)

It was not a pretty grapevine
Along a fence a grape (vine)

B

Todor Todi podvalio
Triput curu poljubio
(Repeat B twice)

Todor tricked Toda
Kissed the girl three times

Verse 3: Lyrics

A

Vec to bese dvoje mili i dragi
Dvoje mili i dragi
(repeat two times)
(Repeat A)

It was, rather, two lovers,
Two lovers

B

Todor Todi podvalio
Triput curu poljubio
(Repeat B twice)

Todor tricked Toda
Kissed the girl three times

VIRGINIA REEL

(ver-jin´-ye re-al)

 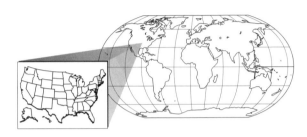

▶ Origin

United States of America

▶ Location

North America, bordered by the Pacific and Atlantic Oceans, and by Canada and Mexico

▶ Language

English

▶ Flag

Thirteen equal horizontal stripes alternating red and white. There is a blue rectangle in the upper-left corner with 50 small white stars in it.

▶ Traditional Costume

(Common folk—mid-19th century) The men wear boots, dark pants, long-sleeved, light-colored shirts, and suspenders. The women wear party dresses or long, full skirts with petticoats and peasant blouses. A bow or ribbon can be worn in the hair.

▶ History of Dance

The Virginia Reel could be thought of as a party game; it's a dance where the dancers made their own music by singing the verses while those on the sidelines joined in by clapping their hands and stamping their feet to the beat. The Virginia Reel actually was adapted from an English dance called Sir Roger de Coverley, and it used to be performed outside on lawns.

▶ Difficulty Level

Easy/moderate

▶ Stance

Relaxed, but somewhat erect. This is a very lively dance!

▶ Music Selection & Time Signature

Fisher's Hornpipe/Turkey in the Straw/Sally Ann Johnson (4/4 time)

▶ Number of Participants

Four to six couples in each set

▶ Formation

Contra. Two lines about four feet apart, partners facing each other.

Head   Foot

Directions

Begin facing partner.

Part 1: Forward and Bow, Walk Back

(8 counts) Walk three steps toward partner, women curtsy and men bow, walk back to place—four steps.

(8 counts) Repeat

Part 2: Right Elbow Swing

(8 counts) Walk two or three steps to partner and join right elbows; turn clockwise in a circle once, and move back to original position.

Part 3: Left Elbow Swing

(8 counts) Walk two or three steps to partner and join left elbows; turn counterclockwise once in a circle and move back to original position.

Part 4: Two Hand Turn

(8 counts) Walk two or three steps to partner and join both hands, turn clockwise once in a circle, and move back to your original position.

Part 5: Do-Si-Do

(8 counts) Walk toward your partner and pass right shoulders, move around each other (back to back), and pass left shoulders as you walk backward to your original position. For added styling, the men may hold their suspender straps at shoulder level with their thumbs, and the women may show off their pretty skirts by swishing them.

Part 6: Sashay Down and Back

(8 counts) Head couple of the set meet in the center, join both hands, and *sashay* (slide) down to the foot (or bottom) of the set.

(8 counts) Head couple of the set sashay back to the top (or head) of the set.

Part 7: Reel the Set

(42 counts) Head couple hook right elbows, turn one and a half times clockwise, then separate. Head man then hooks his left elbow with the next woman-in-line's left elbow while the head woman hooks her left elbow with the next man-in-line's left elbow. These two couples turn counterclockwise once, then separate. Meeting in the middle, the head

couple again hook right elbows, turn once clockwise, separate, then move on and hook left elbows with the next person in line. Repeat this reeling pattern until the head couple reach the foot of the set. The head couple meet in the center, hook right elbows, and turn a half circle to the original side of the set.

(8 counts) Head couple join both hands and sashay back to the top of the set.

Part 8: Cast Off and Follow the Leader

(8 counts) Everyone makes a quarter turn to face the head of the set. The head couple separate, leading each row to the outside, then down the outside of the set to the foot of the set. Each person in line follows the head person in single-file. The head couple join both hands at the foot of the set and raise their hands and arms to form an arch.

Part 9: Arch

(8 to 16 counts) The following couples pair up, walk under the arch, and join both hands as they sashay to the head of the set. (The original head couple is now at the foot, or bottom, of the set, while the second couple in line is the new head, or top, couple).

Repeat the entire dance until all couples have had a chance to be the head couple.

▶ Modifications

- For simplification, you may consider omitting the reeling steps (Part 7). The order would go directly from the sashay down and back (Part 6) to casting off (Part 8), then continuing as described.
- Try it without the music, with a "caller" calling out the steps, such as "forward and bow," and clapping hands.
- Use a variety of music with different tempo changes.

▶ TRIVIA TIDBITS ◀

- This dance was portrayed in the movie *Gone with the Wind*.
- The Virginia Reel was George Washington's favorite dance.

D'HAMMERSCHMIEDSGSELLN
(duh-ham'-mair-shmeets-guh-sehln)

 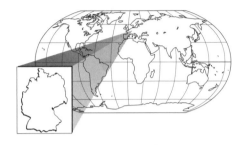

▶ Origin
Germany

▶ Location
Central Europe, bordered by the North Sea, Poland, Austria, and France

▶ Language
German

▶ Flag
Three equal horizontal stripes of black, red, and gold

▶ Traditional Costume
Men wear leather pants called *lederhosen,* which are held up by suspenders (called *trager*) and knee-length socks (*stutzen*), white shirts, and black shoes. Women wear small white tops with a knee-length dress over the top, sometimes with lace or coins attached around the neckline, and eyelet aprons (*dirndl* dresses).

▶ History of Dance
The name of this dance comes from the words *d'hammer* (blacksmith) and *schmiedsgselln* (professional), which translates as "the blacksmith's dance." This dance was originally performed only by men in Bavaria. It is a form of *schuhplattle* dance, part of the dance tradition where men beat rhythms by slapping thighs, shoe soles, and hands. *Plattle* means "slapping" in German.

▶ Difficulty Level
Easy/moderate

▶ Stance
Upright

▶ Music Selection & Time Signature
d'hammerschmiedsgselln (3/4 time)

▶ Number of Participants
Four dancers in each set

▶ Formation
Set of four dancers; two couples, the woman on the man's right with each facing their diagonal opposites (that is, both of the men and both of the women face each other).

Directions

Part 1: Hand Clapping Pattern (*plattle*)

a. The first half of the pattern uses 3 counts and involves clapping various parts of the dancer's body as follows:

(1 count) Clap your hands on your own thighs.

(1 count) Clap your hands on your own rib cage (or stomach).

(1 count) Clap your own hands together.

b. The second half of the pattern uses 3 counts and involves clapping hands with a partner as follows:

(1 count) Clap your partner's right hand with your right hand.

(1 count) Clap your partner's left hand with your left hand.

(1 count) Clap your partner's both hands with both of your hands.

Note: To coordinate the clapping sequence that begins after the music introduction, couple 1 (the women) perform the first half of the pattern, while couple 2 (the men) perform the second half of the pattern. Thus, the men perform the first half of the pattern on the second measure of the music (alternating where they start the sequence). This allows the pattern to mesh with two couples in the set. The entire 6-count pattern is completed eight times in each of Parts 1, 3, and 5.

(42 counts) Repeat hand clapping pattern seven more times and hold on the last 2 counts to make the transition to the next part.

Part 2: Step-Hop Pattern

(48 counts) Everyone joins hands and performs eight step-hops (with a knee lift) while moving clockwise, then repeats in the counterclockwise direction. Couple 1 starts with the right feet while couple 2 starts with the left feet. This step-hop pattern uses sixteen measures of music.

Part 3: Plattle

(48 counts) Repeat the hand clapping pattern from Part 1. Another way to describe these counts is to make eight repetitions of the 6-count plattle.

Part 4: Step-Hop Pattern

(48 counts) Put right hands in the middle to form a star and do eight step-hops while moving clockwise. Then, put left hands in the middle to form a star and do eight step-hops while moving counterclockwise.

Part 5: Plattle

(48 counts) Repeat hand clapping pattern (that is, eight repetitions of the 6-count plattle).

Part 6: Step-Hop Pattern

(48 counts) Repeat eight step-hops with arms in a shoulder-hold position while moving clockwise, then counterclockwise.

▶ Modifications

- Experiment with the hand clapping pattern until everyone feels at ease with the rhythm. Try saying different rhythmic cues for the clapping, such as hit your "thighs, stomach, hands," then "right, left, both (hands)" or clapping in two sets of three's for "**1**, 2, 3" then "**2**, 2, 3", or "me, me, me, you, you, you," or something similar.
- Have partners learn the figure in couples before joining them into the square set.
- Partners may reverse roles in the hand clapping pattern.
- You may repeat the step-hop pattern in Parts 2 and 4 with hands on shoulders.

▶ TRIVIA TIDBITS ◀

- The unification of East Germany and West Germany took place in November 1989, when the Berlin Wall dividing them was taken down.
- Germany has some 4,000 museums, 15,000 libraries (including 9 national libraries), 60 opera houses, 300 other theaters, and more than 150 major orchestras.
- Agriculture plays a minor role in the German economy, and the country imports about one-third of its food.

HIGHLIFE
(hī-līf)

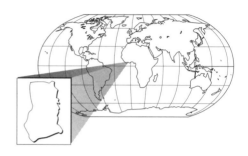

▶ Origin
Ghana

▶ Location
West Africa

▶ Language
Akan, Moshi-Dagomba, Ewe, Ga. English is the official language of Ghana and is universally used in schools.

▶ Flag
Three equal horizontal stripes of red, gold, and green with a black star in the center stripe.

▶ Traditional Costume
Men wear big tops called *dashikis* and baggy pants. Women wear *lapa* skirts (ankle length skirt) and big blouses called *buba*s with *fila*s (cotton head wraps). Both men's and women's costumes are extremely colorful.

▶ History of Dance
The highlife started as a spiritual dance called *juju* and became a social dance around 1924. The spiritual connotations were removed as the dance developed.

▶ Difficulty Level
Easy/moderate

▶ Stance
Loose, easy, and bouncy

▶ Music Selection & Time Signature

Rhythms of the Highlife (2/4 or 4/4 time)

▶ Number of Participants

No limit

▶ Formation

Groups

Directions

Part 1: Step Together (to Both Sides)

Lean forward from waist toward direction traveled. Relax hips.

a. Eight step-and-bring-feet-together moves to right side as follows:

(2 counts) Step the right foot to the right side as elbows lift and arms go out in opposition (imitating sawing) while looking back over the left shoulder. Place the ball of the left foot beside the right foot and push off the floor (transfer weight to ball of left foot), bringing the palms of the hands together in front of the body.

(14 counts) Repeat seven more times to the right side.

b. Eight step-and-bring-feet-together moves to the left side as follows:

(2 counts) Step the left foot to the left side. Place the ball of the right foot beside the left foot and push off (to transfer weight to right foot) while using opposition arms and looking over the right shoulder.

(14 counts) Repeat seven more times to the left side.

c. Four step-and-bring-feet-together moves to the right side as follows:

(8 counts) Repeat the preceding sequence four times to the right side.

d. Four step-and-bring-feet-together moves to the left side as follows:

(8 counts) Repeat the preceding sequence four times to the left side.

Part 2: Two Step (Alternating Step Touches)

a. Eight step touches alternating forward, then backward, as follows:

(4 counts) Turn facing left diagonal, step right foot forward, touch the ball of the left foot beside the right foot (taking two counts). Then, step back onto the left foot and touch the ball of the right foot beside the left foot (taking two counts). Arms are extended to sides with elbows bent and palms up.

(12 counts) Repeat alternating step touches six more times.

b. Eight step touches alternating backward, then forward as follows:

(4 counts) Turn the body a half turn to the right side, then step the right foot back and touch the ball of the left foot beside the right foot (taking two counts). Step the left foot forward, touch the ball of the right foot beside the left foot (taking two counts). Keep the arms extended to the sides.

(12 counts) Repeat alternating step touches six more times. On the last one, turn the body a half turn to the left to face front again.

c. Six step touches, alternating forward and backward, as follows:

(12 counts) Step the right foot forward, touch the ball of the left foot beside the right foot (taking two counts). Step the left foot backward, touch the ball of the right foot beside the left foot (taking two counts).

Part 3: Step Together (to Both Sides)

(16 counts) Repeat (a) from Part 1.

(16 counts) Repeat (b) from Part 1.

(8 counts) Repeat (c) from Part 1.

Part 4: Two Step (Alternating Step Touches)

a. Eight step touches alternating forward, then backward, as follows:

(16 counts) Starting with the left foot, step forward and bring the ball of the right foot beside the left foot (taking two counts). Step backward with the right foot and bring the ball of the left foot beside the left foot (taking two counts). Repeat six more times.

b. Eight step touches alternating backward, then forward, as follows:

(16 counts) Starting with the left foot, step backward and bring the ball of the right foot beside the left foot (taking two counts). Step forward with the right foot and bring the ball of the left foot beside the right foot (taking two counts). Repeat six more times.

Part 5: Prayer Hands, Moving to Left Side

(16 counts) Repeat step-and-bring-feet-together moves while keeping the palms together and alternately touching the left and right shoulders on each count.

Part 6: Prayer Hands, Moving Downward, Then Upward

(8 counts) Let the hips move forward and back as knees bend in order to lower the body. Continue to keep palms in praying position and alternately touch each shoulder on each count.

(8 counts) Same as just described, only gradually straighten knees to rise up.

Part 7: Step Together (to Both Sides)

a. Six step-and-bring-feet-together moves to the right side as follows:

(12 counts) Repeat actions described in (a) of Part 1.

b. Four step-and-bring-feet-together moves to the left side as follows:

(8 counts) Repeat the actions described in (b) of Part 1.

Part 8: Circle Hips

(24 counts) Do 12 hip circles (each taking two counts) as you repeat the step, together moves (starting with the right foot) and rotate counterclockwise in a circle in place. Arms are in a rounded "V" overhead.

Part 9: Shoulder Shake

(2 counts) Step the right foot to the right side and touch the ball of the left foot beside the right foot.

(2 counts) Step the left foot to the left side and touch the ball of the right foot beside the left foot.

(4 counts) Repeat and continue to shake your shoulders.

▶ Modifications

• To simplify, perform just the steps without the arm motions and the rhythmic movements. However, since the rhythm movement is such an important part of the dance, practice isolating different parts of the body in place. For example, just move the head, shoulders, rib cage and hips to the music. Then add these movements to the steps.

• Any combination of the steps described may be used in any order.

• Try every section of the dance in groups of eight counts each for easier memory retention and to shorten the routine.

▶ TRIVIA TIDBITS ◀

• The population of Ghana is divided into more than 50 ethnic groups. The majority of the people are agricultural workers who live on farms or in small villages.

• Ghana's most important crop is cacao, which is produced chiefly in the Ashanti region by small-scale farmers and is used to make chocolate, cocoa, and cocoa butter.

ALUNELUL
(al-loo-náy-loo)

 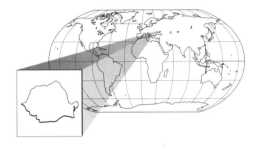

Origin
Romania

Location
Southeastern Europe, bordered by the Black Sea, Bulgaria, Serbia, Hungary, and the Ukraine

Language
Romanian, Hungarian, German

Flag
Three equal vertical stripes of blue, gold, and red

Traditional Costume
Men wear colorful embroidered high-necked tunics with sashes tied at the waist, full pants, and tall black boots. Women wear dresses somewhat fitted at the waist with short decorative vests over the top or waist aprons. They may also wear boots.

History of Dance
Alunelul may also be spelled *alunelu,* and it means "little hazelnut."

Difficulty Level
Easy/moderate

Stance
Upright

▶ Music Selection & Time Signature
Alunelul (4/4 time)

▶ Number of Participants
Circles of eight to ten

▶ Formation
Single circle, all facing the center, hands on the shoulders of the person on either side, or hands held down.

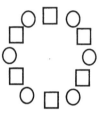

Directions

Note: Stamps do not have a weight change in this dance. For styling, step behind onto the ball of the foot (versus the whole or flat foot). This dance uses whole and half counts of music, which makes it very lively.

Part 1: Double Grapevine With Double Stamp

(4 counts) Face sideways toward the right side to start. Traveling to the right, step on the right foot (on count 1), step on the left foot behind the right foot (on "and" count), step on the right foot (on count 2), step on the left foot behind the right foot (on "and" count), step on the right foot (on count 3), stamp the left heel twice (on "and" count and count 4), and hold for a half count (with no weight change).

(4 counts) Face sideways toward the left side to start. Traveling to the left, step on the left foot (on count 1), step on the right foot behind the left foot (on "and" count), step on the left foot (on count 2), step on the right foot behind the left foot (on "and" count), step on the left foot (on count 3), stamp the right heel twice (on "and" count and count 4), and hold for a half count (with no weight change).

(8 counts) Repeat all of Part 1.

Part 2: Single Grapevine With Single Stamp

(2 counts) Step on the right foot to the right side (on count 1), step on the left foot behind the right foot (on "and" count), step on the right foot (on count 2), and stamp the left heel once (on "and" count).

(2 counts) Step on the left foot to the left side (on count 1), step on the right foot behind the left foot (on "and" count), step on the left foot (on count 2), and stamp the right heel once (on "and" count).

(4 counts) Repeat all of Part 2.

Part 3: Alternating Side Step-and-Stamp With Double Stamp

(4 counts) Moving to the right side, step on the right foot (on count 1), and stamp the left heel (on "and" count). Moving to the left side, step on the left foot (on count 2), and stamp right heel (on "and" count). Then, step on the right foot (on count 3), and stamp the left heel twice (on "and" count and count 4), holding the last half-count.

(4 counts) Repeat, starting to the left side.

▶ Modifications

- To decrease the difficulty, either slow down the tempo or count the dance actions in whole counts (giving each action one beat of music, versus using whole and half beats of music as described).
- Hold the hands low rather than putting hands on shoulders.
- You may find this dance more enjoyable using hard-soled shoes, as opposed to authentic shoes, so you can hear the sounds.

▶ TRIVIA TIDBITS ◀

- Poems, folktales, and folk music have always held a central place in Romanian culture.
- Romanian culture is largely derived from the Roman, with strains of Slavic, Magyar (Hungarian), Greek, and Turkish influence.

YANKO
(yahn-ko')

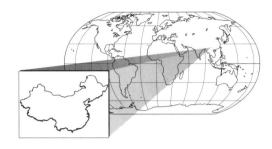

▶ Origin
China

▶ Location
Eastern Asia. Shares a border with Mongolia and Russia in the north, and the Himalayas and South China Sea in the south.

▶ Language
Standard Chinese (Mandarin) is the official language; other dialects include Yue (Cantonese), Wu (Shanghaise), Menbei (Fuzhou), Minnan (Hokkien-Taiwanese), Xiang, Gan, and Hakka.

▶ Flag
Solid red with a large yellow star and four smaller yellow stars in the upper-left corner

▶ Traditional Costume
Men wear lightweight pants and white shirts. Women wear traditional Chinese dresses or pantsuits, usually silk with embroidered designs.

▶ History of Dance
Yanko (ribbon dance) is one of the most theatrical dances in China. It was performed as entertainment for royalty with two long and colorful silk ribbons. It later developed into a folk dance, using one single ribbon, that was performed in the streets during harvest festivals and other celebrations. This dance requires a Chinese ribbon (see Resources section for more information).

▶ Difficulty Level
Moderate

▶ Stance
Upright

▶ Music Selection & Time Signature
Bu Bu Jiao (4/4 time)

▶ Number of Participants
No limit

▶ Formation
Scattered

Directions

Note: To start, hold the end of the bouquet stick (which later unfolds into a long ribbon on a stick) with the bouquet upright in your dominant hand, and let the stick rest in the crook of your elbow. When holding the ribbon in a single hand, the other hand is placed behind the back of the waist.

Part 1: Walking Step

(8 counts) Begin with the right foot. Using a heel, ball, toe motion, walk eight steps forward toward the left front diagonal direction while holding the bouquet in the crook of the right elbow, with the left hand down along side of body. Swing arms naturally to the sides while walking.

(4 counts) Bow as follows: Step on the right foot to the right side, place the ball of the left foot behind the right foot, bend knees to bow, and nod head slightly. Straighten legs, holding the bouquet with both hands by the right hip.

(4 counts) Pose as follows: Step the left foot to the left side, place the right leg across in front of the left leg, and point the right toe. Show the bouquet to the audience by holding it with both hands up above the head, then switch the bouquet to the left hand (leaving the bouquet above the head) and circle the right wrist counterclockwise to point directly out in front of the right shoulder (toward the audience).

Part 2: Peek-a-Boo

(8 counts) Hide your face directly behind the bouquet. Jump up (with both feet off the ground) and tilt land on both feet (sometimes called a bunny hop), and peek out from the right side of the bouquet (using two counts). Then, jump up, land, and peek out from the left side of the bouquet (using two counts). Repeat to alternately peek out from the right and the left sides again (using four counts).

(4 counts) Place the right leg in front and step on the right foot, left foot, and right foot while turning 180 degrees to end facing the back.

(4 counts) Turn 180 degrees to the right by jumping (or "hopping") up in the air for one count, and end facing the front. To release the ribbon, use an overhand throwing motion to throw the bouquet high over head and let the ribbon unfold. Be careful not to throw the stick out of your hand.

Part 3: Figure Eights

(8 counts) Starting with the ribbon in front of the body, make big right arm movements across in front of the body, first to the right, then to the left, in a figure-eight motion. The left hand is out to the side in the butterfly gesture (thumb touching ring finger). Step on the right foot to the right side, then on the left foot to the left side.

Part 4: Running Steps

(8 counts) Use a heel, ball, toe motion and a fast tempo during the running steps. With the ribbon on the left of the body, move the right hand up and down in large wave motions while running to the right side (using 6 counts). There should be two running steps for each count of music; for example, step on the right foot on count 1, and step on the left foot on the "and" count. On counts 7 and 8, throw the ribbon to the right side of the body while placing the left leg behind the right leg.

(8 counts) Repeat Part 4, running to the left.

Part 5: Circle With Running Steps

(8 counts) Bring the ribbon up and behind the head and wave it by moving the ribbon to the right and left sides. Place the left hand (with palm facing out) behind the waist. Complete eight running steps to the right in a small circle while waving the ribbon behind the head.

Part 6: Half Peaches

(8 counts) Hold the ribbon down at your right side. With the right foot in front of the left foot, rise up on your toes and lift the ribbon up to the sky (by bringing the right arm up from along the side of the body) using one count. Then, bring the right arm down as heels again touch the floor on count 2. Lift the chin as the body rises, then look straight ahead. The left hand is rotated and behind the waist. Repeat three more times.

Part 7: Half Peaches With Quarter Turns

(8 counts) Repeat Part 6 while turning one quarter turn to the right with each half peach. (You should be facing front after four quarter turns).

Part 8: Moving Figure Eights

(8 counts) Repeat figure eights as in Part 3.

(4 counts) Add the following foot pattern: Step on the right foot to the right side, cross the left foot over the right foot, step on the right foot to the right side, and hop on the right foot with the left leg extended to the side. Make a big circle with the ribbon in front, then a big circle to the side on the hop.

(4 counts) Repeat in opposition to the left side with the left foot.

(4 counts) Repeat to the right side.

(4 counts) Repeat to the left side.

Part 9: Backward Running Steps

(8 counts) Start on the right foot and complete eight running steps to the right side while moving backward and circling the ribbon in front in small, figure-eight circles.

Part 10: Turn

(8 counts) Turn 360 degrees to the right while waving the ribbon up and down with the right arm.

Part 11: Ending Posture

(4 counts) Bow (as in Part 1) by stepping on the right foot, placing the ball of the left foot behind the right foot, and bending the knees. Nod the head slightly. Keep the ribbon beside the right hip.

(4 counts) Pose (as in Part 1).

Note: To have the dance fit the music, complete the parts in the following order:

Parts 1, 2, 3, 4, 5, 6, 7, 8, 9, 3, 4, 5, 6, 7, 8, 9, 3, 4, 5, 6, 7, 8, 9, 10, 11

▶ Modifications

- Substitute a sideward gallop (versus cross) in the second half of Part 8.
- Interchange different groups of dancers so that some move offstage while others move onstage during Parts 3 through 10. This increases the difficulty and lets more dancers participate.
- Try the dance using two ribbons at once.

▶ TRIVIA TIDBITS ◀

- A Chinese checkerboard has 121 holes.
- More than one-fifth of the world's total population live within China's borders.

EL JARABE TAPATIO
(el ha-rah'-bee tah-pah-ti'oh)

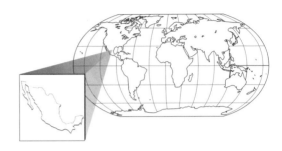

▶ Origin
Mexico

▶ Location
Middle America, bounded by the Pacific Ocean and the Gulf of Mexico

▶ Language
Spanish

▶ Flag
Three equal vertical bands of green, white, and red, with the Mexican coat of arms (an eagle perched on a cactus with a snake in its beak) in the center band

▶ Traditional Costume
The costumes that are worn by both men and women are decreed to represent Mexico. The man wears a black *charro* suit with a large black hat. The pants are tight fitting and have decorations such as horseshoes or aztec symbols along the sides, from the waist to just above the bottom of the pants. The top is a short, trimmed bolero jacket, shirt, and short ribbon bow tie. The woman wears the beautiful *China Poblana,* consisting of a brightly colored blouse with exquisite embroidery and a skirt embroidered with sequins depicting the national symbol, an eagle perched on a cactus with a snake in its beak. A cummerbund is worn around the waist and ribbons ornament the hair.

▶ History of Dance

This is a dance that by national decree represents the nation of Mexico to the world. *El Jarabe Tapatio* (The Mexican Hat Dance) is the interpretation of a woman's flirtations toward a man and a man's courtship of a woman in which love blooms. It originated in central Mexico, near the state of Jalisco. The dance was composed of dance figures from all over central Mexico dating back perhaps 200 years.

▶ Difficulty Level

Advanced

▶ Stance

Somewhat erect—with confidence. The man clasps his hands behind his back, and the woman holds her skirt.

▶ Music Selection & Time Signature

El Jarabe Tapatio (4/4; then 3/4; then 4/4 time)

▶ Number of Participants

No limit

▶ Formation

Partners facing each other

Directions

Introduction

The dance begins with the couple facing each other with arms crossed (right arm over left arm) and holding hands. Both partners release their left hands as the man lifts his right arm to lead the woman's counterclockwise turn under his arm. Facing each other, they release right hands and move back away from each other.

Part 1: Walk Forward and Back

(4 counts) Both dancers start with their right foot and walk toward each other as follows: Step right foot, left foot, right foot, and tap the left toe in back of the right foot. Both partners angle their right shoulders forward on the back tap.

(4 counts) Both dancers walk backward, starting with their left foot, as follows: Step left foot, right foot, left foot, and end with a toe tap in front of the left foot. Both partners angle their right shoulders backward on the front tap.

(8 counts) Repeat Part 1.

Part 2: Paseo (Basic Step)

(1-and-a counts) Both dancers step on their right foot with flat foot, dig the heel of the left foot, and step on the right foot with flat foot.

(1-and-a counts) Step on the left foot, dig the heel of the right foot, and step on the left foot.

(14 counts) Repeat paseo (basic step) on both sides of the body 14 more times. To add styling, both dancers may rotate to face one side, then the other side while doing the basic step.

Part 3: Paso Lazadas (Roping Step)

(2 counts) Both dancers step their left foot forward while lifting the right leg in a counterclockwise, circular motion (heel lift occurs on count 2), then quickly step on the right foot in front.

(14 counts) Repeat seven more times while traveling clockwise and add two stomps on counts 15 and 16.

(16 counts) Repeat Part 3.

Part 4: El Ermate

(2 counts) Both dancers step on their left foot, scuff the right heel forward and brush back, step on the right foot, then step on the left foot.

(12 counts) Repeat six more times, alternating sides.

(2 counts) Stomp the right foot, then the left foot (on counts 15 and 16).

Part 5: Paseo (Basic Step)

(16 counts) Perform Paseo (flat, heel, flat) 16 times.

Part 6: Kick, Kick, Fold, Stomp, Stomp

Note: Music changes to 3/4 time here.

(6 counts) Both dancers walk forward, passing right shoulders, as follows: Kick the right leg and step on the right foot (on count 1). Kick the left leg and step on the left foot (on count 2). On count 3, fold the right ankle over by rotating the right foot such that the outside of the

ankle bears the weight change—do this with caution! If there is any potential problem, substitute a cross step. Turn clockwise to face each other, and step on the left foot, then stomp the right foot (on counts 4 and 5). Hold on count 6 (prepare to start with the right foot again).

(6 counts) Repeat Part 6.

Part 7: El Tornillo (Kicking and Twisting of Ankle)

(3 counts) Both dancers scuff their right heel forward, stomp the right foot, dig the left heel with the foot turned inward, and stomp on the right, then left foot.

(12 counts) Repeat four more times as both dancers rotate around each other.

(3 counts) Stomp right foot, then left foot, and hold.

Part 8: Full Turn

(1-and counts) As you are turning clockwise, step on the right foot and push with the ball of the left foot.

(2 counts) Repeat step and push two more times.

(3 counts) Stomp the right foot and hold.

(36 counts) Repeat Parts 6, 7, and 8.

Part 9: El Boracho

(3 counts) Both dancers move side to side and pass right shoulders while performing the following footwork: Stomp the right foot, step on the left foot (placed behind the right foot), step on the right foot in place. This is sometimes called a *triple step,* as three weight changes occur.

(3 counts) Do another triple step, starting with the left foot, as follows: Stomp on the left foot, step on the right foot (placed behind the left foot), and step on the left foot in place.

(9 counts) Repeat the footwork just described three more times and turn to face each other on the last one.

(3 counts) Stomp the right foot, then the left foot.

(6 counts) Walk backward away from each other with the right foot, left foot, right foot, and stomp the left foot. As an alternative, the backward walks may be done with the ankle rolled outward on each step.

Part 10: El Paso Atole

(6 counts) Both dancers walk toward each other doing a kick-type step, as follows: Kick the right foot (on count 1) and quickly step on the right foot, kick the left foot (on count 2) and quickly step on the left foot, kick the right foot (on count 3) and quickly step on the right foot, and add a small jump to land on both feet (on count 4). Lift the right leg and turn the right foot and lower leg inward twice (counter-clockwise, circular motion on counts 5 and 6).

(6 counts) Repeat the preceding steps while passing partner's right shoulder.

(6 counts)With backs to each other, do two modified triple steps, as follows: (a) Stomp the right foot in place, then step on the right foot, step on the ball of the left foot (placed behind the right foot), step the right foot in place, and (b) stomp the left foot in place, step on the left foot, step on the ball of the right foot (placed behind the left foot), and step the left foot in place.

(3 counts) Turn 180 degrees to face each other while continuing the footwork: stomp the right foot, step on the right foot, step on the ball of the left foot (placed behind the right foot), and stomp the right foot.

(3 counts) Step and push twice and stomp.

▶ Modifications

- Practice the dance to a slower tempo.
- Perform the steps without the turns.
- Perform the steps on each count and delete the partial counts.
- Because this dance is difficult, practice only one part at a time and slowly add on.

▶▶ TRIVIA TIDBITS ◀

- The distinctive folk songs and dances heard in various regions of Mexico are accompanied by several kinds of guitar-based ensembles. The *mariachi,* or popular strolling bands, consist of a standard group of instruments: two violins; two five-string guitars; a guittarón, or large bass guitar; and usually a pair of trumpets.

- Tortillas are an important food for most Mexican people. They are made from maize (corn), Mexico's leading crop.

Teaching multicultural folk dancing is an exciting adventure. You have an opportunity to meet all types of wonderful people and help them learn about themselves and each other through movement. Whether you are an experienced teacher or just getting started, here are some teaching techniques to assist you in your endeavors.

The essence of folk dancing is found in the spirit of each dancer and in the atmosphere that permeates the group. Thus, attention should be given to making the students feel comfortable and successful. A good educator should "feel" the group, which is an art in itself.

Suggestions for successful class formats include opening each class by sharing some information about the country. The history of the dance gives meaning and spirit to the instruction. For the first class, have students introduce themselves to each other. Teach a dance that does not require a partner, such as the Hora. Play the music a few times and have the class clap their hands to the beat. Increase the bass on the sound system if anyone is having trouble hearing the beat of the music. It is advisable to have a sound system with a speed control so you are able to increase and decrease the tempo of the music to adjust to the class environment.

Always play music, even if the volume is low. It is a great motivator and creates a feeling for the country. The body needs to be warmed up gradually, so have the dancers walk in place in time to the music. Then they can walk forward and back and side to side. After the first class, you can actually warm up the students by reviewing a dance they have already learned. Just remember to walk through the dance slowly and gradually increase the tempo.

Once you have warmed up the group, introduce the new dance. Begin by teaching the easiest moves to increase their self confidence. Review parts of the dance that may require more attention. Repeat the sections numerous times. Then teach the entire dance, paying special attention to correct terminology. If the dance is a circle dance, you may find it easier to teach it in a straight line first without having students hold hands. Be sure to tell students about the formation of the dance (circle, lines, squares, etc.), the direction of the dance (clockwise or counterclockwise) and which foot to start on.

The progressive method of teaching is a great technique. First, teach Part 1 of a selected dance. Once Part 1 is taught, have the students perform it first without the music, then with the music at a slow speed, and then increase the speed to the correct tempo. When they have performed Part 1 successfully, teach Part 2. After they have danced Part 2 successfully, add Part 1 and Part 2 together. Then teach Part 3. Continue on until all the parts are taught and the dance is completed.

Memorize your directions and calls. It is important for you to "cue" your dancers ahead of time. For example, on the 5th count of an 8 count, you can say, "Get ready to step right!" This takes practice, but is extremely helpful to the dancer. Make sure that you clarify when you are cueing the footwork (weight changes taken) or when you are cueing the beats of the music. For example, a triple step takes three weight changes within two beats of music. If the footwork actions are called out "1, 2, 3," then the students may think that this is the timing with the music when it is not.

When teaching moves that step side to side, turn and face the students and teach in opposition. A back to the audience is not as exciting as your smiling face, good projection, and enthusiasm. When teaching step patterns that move forward and back from the student, it is essential that you teach with your back toward them so they can follow your lead. When teaching partner dances, have partners face each other while you face your partner so you create a mirror image to the students before trying a dance formation. End each class with the students' choice of dance or with an old favorite. At the end of a high-energy dance, have the students walk around in a circle to cool down instead of abruptly stopping.

Some ideas for partner dances if you have more women than men (or vice versa) is to designate partners by other means. For example, give the "female" roles a color ("all the reds go over here") and give the "male" roles a different color. Maybe you can provide a colored arm band using ribbons or scarves. In addition, you can use gender-neutral terms to describe the different roles, for example, separate the dancers according to the formation (refer to the "inner circle dancers" and the "outer circle dancers") to avoid male/female gender references while teaching unequal groups. Challenge the dancers to perform a role versus "do the man's part (or the woman's part). While teaching dances that require a partner, it is always helpful to change partners frequently.

In planning a unit, keep in mind the students' ages, ability levels, the length of the class, and the number of lesson periods available. Every class will be different. Modify, modify, modify to fit your class! If *you* can't do it, chances are, *they* can't! Maybe you will get a class that is very coordinated and learns fast. Then you will need to challenge them by teaching faster, adding turns, and increasing tempo. The biggest test is when you have mixed ability levels in a class. A good solution to this situation is to teach to the beginning level and give the advanced dancers more advanced steps or modifications to perform during the same amount of time.

Always remember the main objective of folk dance is fun and fellowship. In dance everyone is a winner and students should feel very good about themselves. As a teacher, you can help create this feeling. Remember to have students warm up gradually and be sure to have them cool down correctly. Create images and cues that students' minds can adapt to easily. (Be sure to give the mind a "breather" before teaching a new step.) The students will feel good about themselves if they can successfully dance the progressions. They will feel comfortable around each other because of your positive teaching methods. All of this will create the atmosphere needed to let their spirits shine through and allow them to feel the real joy of multicultural folk dancing.

RESOURCES

▶ Dance Instructors (Volume 1)

Alexandru David (Romania)
P.O. Box 139
Tarzana, CA 91356

Rosina Didyk (Serbia)
Aman Folk Ensemble
P.O. Box 90593
Long Beach, CA 90809
(213) 931-1750

Richard Duree (Germany)
Dance Traditions
P.O. Box 1642
Costa Mesa, CA 92628
(714) 641-7450

Gal Haas (Israel)
Keshet Chain Dance Ensemble
10430 Wilshire Blvd, #1704
Los Angeles, CA 90024
(310) 441-1719

Lynnanne Hanson (USA)
732 Brent Avenue
South Pasadena, CA 91030
(626) 441-0260

Christy Lane
Christy Lane Enterprises
P.O. Box 4040
Palm Springs, CA 92263-4040
(800) 555-0205

Susan A. C. Langhout
P.O. Box 606
Bemidjio, MN 56619
(218) 755-2941

Nipo Lauri (Hawaii)
Le Polynesia
8111 Token Street
Long Beach, CA 90808
(562) 596-3226

Olivia Liou (China)
1300 Cascade Avenue
Walnut, CA 91789
(909) 595-1999

Enrique Rodriguez (Mexico)
6215 Allston Street
Los Angeles, CA 90022
(213) 728-8331

Lady Walquer (Ghana)
The Dance Collective
4327 Degnan Blvd
Los Angeles, CA 90008
(213) 273-9914

▶ Equipment

For tambourines, hula skirts, Hawaiian leis, tinikling sticks, sombreros, and country flags, contact

Christy Lane Enterprises
P.O. Box 4040
Palm Springs, CA 92263-4040
(800) 555-0205

Complete your set!

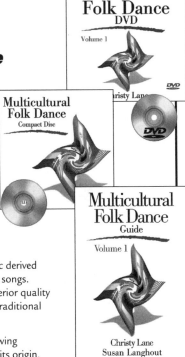

2335

You'll find other outstanding
dance resources at
www.HumanKinetics.com